101 Writing Prompts for Fantasy and Science Fiction Writers

Volume 1

By L. K. Grant

Text copyright © 2012 L. K. Grant
Cover art copyright © 2012 Geoffrey A. Pratt
Cover design copyright © 2012 L. K. Grant

*for the sweet ladies and gents
from various writing groups
who were kind enough to be my guinea pigs*

*for Geoff Rugg,
who opened his heart and home to me
and who gave me reason to hope again*

*and for Jo Carson
who is with me still as I pass
by all these damn dragons*

~ 4 ~

Table of Contents

Dedication	3
Table of Contents	5
Preface	6
Using These Prompts	7
Prompts	10
Thanks	50

Preface

Dear Writer,

I wanted this book to be more than just a list of writing prompts, though it certainly delivers that.

I hope to show you, a writer of speculative and outlandish fiction, a way of generating your own prompts for fantasy and sci-fi stories using history, personal and anecdotal experiences, and the fascinating origins of common words and phrases.

Many pages of this book offer not just a prompt but also the seed of the prompt, showing you how I have used reality to create reality-bending story ideas.

I have tried to derive many of these prompts from real science, real experiences and real people. Truly engaging fantasy, science and speculative fiction all contain one thing: a grain of truth. When readers sense verisimilitude, they will let you take them to fascinating new worlds.

They will believe everything you tell them.

Using These Prompts

If you downloaded this book, chances are you already know how writing prompts work. But as a refresher, here are a few tips.

Give each prompt at least five minutes of solid writing. If you find yourself writing for a couple of hours as the result of one prompt, great! Some of them may even lead you to complete stories or novels, and if that happens, awesome. But give your brain a chance to kick in to gear with each one. Even if you sit in front of the computer for four and a half minutes with nothing of worth coming out, you are giving your brain a workout. Your brain is like you probably were in high school: it gets bored in class and starts to daydream. While daydreams got you in trouble when you were a teenager, they are *exactly* what your brain should be doing when you sit down to write.

With many prompts, I ask several questions. Feel free to answer some, all or none of them.
Many writers use prompts to get the creative juices flowing before sitting down to the hard slog of writing. Others use prompts to give their brain some relief, especially if they find themselves stuck within a longer piece of fiction. With this in mind, I have written a lot of these prompts with "your character"

as the main subject, so that you can take your protagonist out of the novel/story you are currently working on and plop him/her down in another setting, just to shake things up a bit and see what happens. If you're just writing to get the aforementioned juices flowing, this may be a great way for you to 'meet' new characters, characters that may decide that you are the one to write their story.

Some pages provide simply a strange or underused word and its definition. The dictionary is a great place to find inspiration, and for these prompts I suggest that you try one of several methods: write the word into a scene, use the word as the title of a book or story, or use the word as a name for a new character and write about that character, showing how that character does (or doesn't) live up to the name.

Good luck, and please feel free to contact me at any time. I'd love to see what comes of these prompts and answer any questions you might have.

~Laura
LKeenerGrant@gmail.com

~ 10 ~

1

There is a village in West Africa known as the Land of Twins because an unusually large number of twins are born there, nearly four times the global average. Additionally, some scientists say that this high rate of twins is caused by the local diet, specifically yams that contain a hormone that causes a woman to release two eggs at once.

Imagine a place called the Land of Twins, where everyone is somebody's twin. Now imagine that there is one person who was born with no twin. What would their life be like? Would they be ostracized or worshipped?

For a new twist, imagine a food that creates such a noticeable effect. Think beyond yams and multiple births: what other aspects of birth would people want to control? What kind of food could control this?

2

Gyrfalcon, n: (also gerfalcon, from *gerfaucun, girfaucon, gyrofalco*) an arctic falcon that occurs in several forms, is the largest of all falcons, and is more powerful, though less active, than the peregrine falcon. Their wingspans can reach 5-6 feet, and their eggs look like dark gold stones.

In the 12th Century, a Chinese Emperor demanded gyrfalcons as tax, seeing just how profitable the birds were as hunting companions. The rebellion of tribes unwilling to hand over their falcons led to a new dynasty.

Imagine a rebellion with falconers using their birds as weapons. What sights and sounds would your character see on the battlefield?

For a new twist: many rebellions involve some level of skulduggery. How could rebels use falcons in subterfuge?

3

Blood oranges gain their eponymous color overnight, and only when the night is cold. They are sometimes called vampire oranges.

Imagine an orchard tended by vampires (or a similar night-dwelling creature). What kind of fruit would these creatures grow? What special properties or powers could it have? How would they defend it during the day? What about a fruit that has certain properties when harvested during the day and quite different properties when harvested at night? Eaten during the day vs. at night?

4

In 2010, Lady's Slipper orchids were found on a golf course in the U.K. Because they are endangered, and because they fetch a high price for poachers, local police were dispatched to guard them around the clock while they were blooming.

Imagine a plant so valuable that it had to be guarded by force. What properties (or even powers) could it possess? Write about one of the guards. Write about a poacher.

A new twist: what if the guards weren't protecting the flowers from people, but instead people from the flowers?

5

Your character has to bathe in ocean water every day. Twenty-two hours have passed since he/she has been to the ocean. The car won't start, and walking takes too long.

Does he/she make it? Why does he/she have to get there, and what happens if he/she doesn't?

6

Write about a kid who discovers that he has the ability to read minds...while in sex ed class. How many different 'voices' can you bring to life through his mind?

7

Your character wakes up on a park bench in a big city, surrounded by joggers, moms, old ladies, dogs, and a cop or two. He/she has no clothes and no memory of the past 12 hours, although there was a full moon the night before...

8

A man has to convince a young princess, who is eleven, not to behead his brother. The setting is a court in a castle, with members of the court looking on.

Now change up the genders and ages of the characters. How do the dynamics shift? Try this scenario with at least three different sets of characters.

9

Your character gets into a carriage headed out of a village. In his/her satchel is a very special package. What is it, how did he/she get it, where is he/she going, and does he/she make it alive...

10

...you character gets onto a subway car in a metro area. In his/her briefcase is a very special package. What is it, how did he/she get it, where is he/she going, and does he/she make it alive?

11

Your character has to spend the night sleeping in a tree after two days of running from the King's guards. He/she awakens to find that the guards have set up camp beneath his tree, but do not seem to know he's up there. What happens next?

12

In a small house on the outskirts of town, a brilliant but underfunded and unrecognized botanist lives and works. One morning, he heads out to his greenhouse, where something unexpected has blossomed overnight. As he enters, describe: what he smells, hears, sees, etc. Who will he tell first? How will this discovery change him, and the world he lives in?

13

Your character has a Polaroid camera that can photograph ghosts. How does he/she use it to get out of a sticky situation?

14

Your character's escape pod has landed on a strange planet. As he/she watches his/her ship disintegrate outside the planet's atmosphere, he/she struggles to set up a communication tower quickly to signal the mother ship. This planet has some notoriously hostile inhabitants.

15

Two men have just kidnapped a twelve-year-old for ransom. Little do these abductors know about their victim's secret ability.

16

Coral inflates and deflates itself to move around and get out of sticky situations.

Your character also has this ability. Send him/her out on a blind date that goes badly. Now send him/her to Thanksgiving dinner. Have a cop pull him/her over.

While writing, be sure to use your descriptive powers to help your reader know what is looks like, sounds like, smells like, etc., when your character inflates/deflates.

17

Harlequin ladybugs were imported to Europe to help with pest control, but now they are nudging out the native species of ladybug.

Your character is a native ladybug, and he/she discovers that all the other ladybugs in the neighborhood are the alien species. How does he/she react? Does he/she fight back? Does he/she shut the blinds, drink his/her tea and reminisce about the old days?

Interesting words to utilize: Harlequin (a comic servant); Ladybird (the European name for ladybugs)

18

Your character has an outer shell, and it secretes a substance that is defensively toxic—but only when he/she eats well. What kind of environment makes this defense necessary? If there is a dearth of food, what will your character do to fend off the enemies chasing him/her?

19

Scientists have discovered a massive lake in the arctic beneath a mile of ice. When they send down an exploratory team (including your character), the sonar and other navigational equipment begins to pick up strange signals. Just out of reach of the seacraft's lights, something enormous looms.

20

Your character stumbles upon a large nest with three huge eggs in it. He/she stops to look at them because they appear so strange. He/she notices two sounds: a tapping noise from inside one of the eggs, and the sound of air moving behind.

21

Your character's horse has expired, so it's time to buy a new one. Locals say that the farrier down the lane may have one for sale. When your character gets there, he/she is not immediately impressed by the look of the horse, but for such a low price…

22

Your character is making a name for him/herself as a professional fighter (or if you prefer, an underground fighter), and it's all thanks to the injections he/she gets everyday from Dr. Huckenspud's latest experiment. He/she is winning a lot of money, but the side effects are quite strange.

23

One morning in Ms. Fuller's science class, a simple experiment produces an unexpected burst of greenish red smoke. None of her students seem hurt, but she begins to notice that they're exhibiting some strange behaviors.

24

Goatsucker, n: any of a family of medium-sized long-winged crepuscular or nocturnal birds having a short, wide bill, short legs, and soft mottled plumage, and feeding on insects that they catch on the wing.

Write about a goat that is afraid of birds. This is a chance to anthropomorphize in the extreme, so give him a house to live in, a car to drive, and a rabid fear of birds.

25

Your character pauses at the bank of a small stream to fill his/her goatskin. Suddenly he/she notices a small fox sitting on its haunches on the opposite bank. They watch each other for a moment. Then the fox speaks.

26

Fracas, n: a noisy quarrel, brawl

27

swarm spore, n: any of various minute motile sexual or asexual spores

28

Your character has found a way to bottle stardust, and brings back a bottle of it to his/her town. When a beautiful woman buys it and rubs it onto her skin, something unexpected happens.

29

Several characters are feasting on a hillside in honor of a) a victory in battle, b) an ascension by one of their number to the position of chief or king, or c) a wedding/birthday. Suddenly a ghibli (a hot desert wind) hearkens the approach of a massive storm. Write a two paragraph scene.

Now write the ghibli as a character, with human emotions and senses. How does this feast look to your ghibli?

30

rhumb, n: any of the points of the mariner's compass

31

Your character falls asleep and dreams of a man sprinkling sand over his/her eyes. Upon awakening, he/she is no longer where he/she fell asleep. A gritty, white sand falls from your character's eyes as he/she takes in the new surroundings. Describe the dream.

32

samara, n: a dry, one-seeded winged fruit (as of an ash, elm or maple tree) —also called a key

Your character approaches a tree, an old, very thick tree, and sees a door carved in the trunk. The elf/forest creature/nymph that sent your character here said that the key would be on the ground beneath the tree, but all your character sees are tiny seedpods, which he/she knows are called samara...

33

sangfroid, n: self-possession, especially under strain, from the French for "cold blood"

34

squamation, n: the state of being scaly. the arrangement of scales on an animal

Use this as the first sentence: "At first, all _____ could see was a vague, gray squamation filling his/her vision and moving in and out of focus, as if something very large was breathing..."

35

Tree surgeons trim trees, cutting branches in such a way that helps the tree grow healthier by controlling decay and preventing the spread of disease.

Imagine a character that takes this title to the extreme, performing more delicate and intense operations on trees. Perhaps the tree is capable of feeling the 'surgery,' or even speaking.

Now imagine a species of tree that becomes powerful or dangerous as it grows. Who does the local village send out to trim the wild wood?

36

yurt, n: a circular domed tent of skins or felt stretched over a collapsible lattice framework and used by Mongol nomads of Siberia

Your character awakens in his/her yurt, which is warm and smells like breakfast. A quick peek out the door flap confirms that it snowed again last night. In the distance, something strange: a lone man on horseback, riding as fast as he can towards the yurt, as though the hounds of hell were close on his heels…

37

Yggdrasil, n: a huge ash tree in Norse mythology that overspreads the world and binds earth, hell and heaven together.

A tree this large could (and does) fill many books, but for this prompt, just write about your character as he/she transitions from one of the three places to another via the tree: earth to hell, heaven to earth, hell to heaven, etc. Why the shift? What does he/she see along the way? What are the physical sensations? Emotional? Spiritual? Who does he/she encounter? Does the past come back to haunt him/her?

38

youngberry, n: the large, sweet, reddish-black fruit of a hybrid between a trailing blackberry and a southern dewberry, grown in western and southern U.S.

Your character is old, and by chance stumbles upon a youngberry bush, and eats a few berries. You decide: does he/she know the effect the berries will have?

He/she begins to grow young. Is it fast or slow, does it hurt or feel amazing? How do others react?

39

Your character is outside with a friend, hunting (or another pastime/task of your choice). A sudden cloudburst comes over them. Before they have time to find shelter, the rain washes away the disguise worn by the friend, revealing his/her startling true identity: the sworn enemy of your character. Who is he/she? How does your character react?

Now switch this. Your character is fighting his/her sworn enemy when their disguise falls away to reveal your character's dearest friend.

40

Your character awakens in a hospital to find that his/her left arm and leg have been replace with robotic limbs, and no memory of the surgery. Your character is horrified by the loss of limbs, but fascinated too, because the limbs seem to respond directly to his/her thoughts.

Now bring in a nurse or doctor, who tells your character what happened—or doesn't, your choice.

41

darkle, v: to become concealed in the dark; to become cloudy or gloomy

Your character has the ability to hide in the shadows. He/she uses this ability to follow a queen and her lover as they discuss murdering the king.

42

daughter, n: an atomic species that is the immediate product of the radioactive decay of a given element

43

dead letter, n: a letter that is undeliverable and unreturnable by the post office

Your character works in the dead letter department, night shift. One night, a bin of dead letters arrives, and as your character sorts through and prepares to destroy them, one of the letters begins to glow and grow warm to the touch.

44

Apple names make great character names, as well as great titles. Looking below, choose two names to put together (like Ashworth Foxwhelp), and then take five minutes to write about your new character. Do this three more times, at least.

Now pick a name (or two) from below and use it as your title. Write for five minutes at least, and see where the story goes.

Abbondanza	Dulsis	Laxton's Fortune	Tolman
Alamanka	Egremont	Lemoine	Tremlett
Ashmead	Redstream	Levering Limbertwig	Turley
Ashworth	Fallawater	Lord Lambourne	Nestor
Beating Hammer	Flower of Kent	Macoun	Newell
Beautiful Arcade	Foxwhelp	Maidstone	Oratia
Belle of Boskoop	Freeborn Jonared	Maigold	Rosthern
Black Mac	Goldspur	Penrome	Rustycoat
Blue Pearmain	Greene Spy	Quindell	Sir Prise
Bramley	Hereford Redstreak	Astrachan	Stark Earliblaze
Buckley Giant	Red Cortland	Rosilda	Vandevere
Cheal's Golden Gem	Holdfast	Scarlet Crofton	Wismer
Chehalis	Honora	Signe Tillisch	Zalesak
Delawine	Idared	Starking	Zeeland
Densmore	Jonwin	Talman	Zorza
Derman	Keswick Codlin	Taunton Cross	

45

One of the lunar plains is named Hell. Your character works at a space station built in Hell, along with about 200 other astronauts, scientists and moon colonists. Your character is in the cafeteria when the power suddenly goes off. Out the giant windows of the cafeteria, the Earth is slowly setting at the moon's far horizon. Soon, it will be out of sight completely.

46

Rhinotillexomania, n: an uncontrollable urge to pick one's nose.

47

cortege, n: a train of attendants, a retinue

Your character is in the cortege of the king, behind about twenty knights, lords and other members of the kings court. He/she has one task: protect the king from assassination.

48

Your character is mining cadmium on a distant planet. Like the other men and women in the mineshaft, your character misses his/her significant other, the sight of the twin suns that this plant circles, and the feel of a cool breeze coming off of the glacial lake he/she lives near. Your character has been working underground for two weeks, and has only five hours and thirty-five minutes to go before work is over. What could possibly go wrong?

49

Your character is exploring a jungle on a distant planet, a place that until now was unseen by human eyes. He/she spies a strange sight: the nuptial plumage of a huge bird, called an Alamanka Macoun (see what I did there?), nearly twice the size of your character. Though not much is known about the Alamanka Macoun, they are known for being very aggressive, especially during mating season…

50

Your character, who is the mayor of Hometown, wakes up one morning to find that Nextdoorville, the sister city of Hometown, has completely disappeared. Though the missing town is only ten miles away from Hometown, no one remembers hearing anything the night before. What does your character do next?

51

Your character is at the beach, walking along the shore, when he/she spies a bright object shining in the sand. The sun is setting/rising, yet the object seems to glow with its own bright warmth.

52

Your character is walking down a road when he/she finds a long bundle laying in the ditch. Upon opening the bundle, he/she finds a sword...

53

Your character is walking down the sidewalk when a car suddenly jumps the curb and barrels toward him/her. He/she reaches on arm out, grabs the bumper and stops the car in its tracks.

54

Your character dreams that he/she can fly, and wakes up floating two feet above the bed.

55

A young girl walks through a forest collecting herbs and roots in a basket. As the day grows dark, she heads home, where her mother has a large, bubbling cauldron hanging over a great fire.

56

A family is eating dinner when they hear a loud thud on the roof. They go outside and find a woman with butterfly wings lying next to the house, unconscious.

57

Your character has heard that the old woman at the end of the lane makes the strongest armor in the realm. She uses a magic spell to swear everyone who comes to her to secrecy, though, so no one has been able to replicate her armor. Your character enters her shop, promises never to tell, and orders a suit of armor. She tells him/her to stand in the middle of the room, within a chalk circle on the floor, and then brings out a wooden box the size of a loaf of bread. There is a strange clicking noise coming from the box. When she opens the lid, a huge spider, the size of a house cat, crawls out and begins to weave a suit of armor over your character.

58

On the outskirts of the village, there is a field where nothing will grow, neither crops nor weeds. Your character is walking past the field one day when he/she notices a small, bright green seedling pushing up through the soil. As he/she approaches it, it seems to grow before his/her eyes.

59

On the same night that a mysterious stranger rolls into town, everyone above the age of twenty-seven loses all of their hair, including eyebrows and beards.

60

For a science project, a sixth grade boy designs a car that can run on water. He comes home with a first place ribbon from the science fair to find his parents missing and two men in dark suits and sunglasses sitting in his living room.

61

Your character gets into his/her car one morning to go to work and notices a big red button on the dashboard that wasn't there before. It blinks at him/her invitingly.

62

The light is dying. In a few moments, the sun will be behind the horizon. Your character is running as fast as he/she can through the streets, but every door is barred, every window boarded up. He/she knows that people can see and hear him/her calling for help, but no one will open their door and offer shelter. The sun finally slips below the horizon.

63

Your character has just spent his last dime on three beans in a plain white paper package. The man who sold him/her the beans swore up and down that they would bring him/her great wealth. Your character is having some severe regret about the impulse buy, but plants the three beans in a small hole in the front yard that night anyway. The next morning, a glimpse out the window reveals a shocking sight.

64

Your character comes home from work one afternoon to find an extra door in the living room. When he/she opens the door, he/she beholds a spiral staircase winding upwards.

Now write it as if the staircase wound down.

65

H.M.R. (His Royal Majesty) Rex-Goliath — a 47-pound rooster belonging to a Texas circus, purported to be the largest rooster on record.

A small girl lives on the farm where Rex Goliath was hatched and raised. She longs to get away from her cruel parents. One day, while feeding the chickens, she hops on R.G.'s, and he starts to run.

66

The first sentence of a story or novel is vitally important. It sets the tone, grabs the reader and pulls her kicking and screaming into the story.

For this prompt, grab a stack of fantasy or sci-fi novels off of your bookshelf. If you have a collection of short stories, that will work just fine.

Write down the last sentence of a story chosen at random from the novels/collections you gathered together, and then use it as the first sentence of a new piece. Write for at least five minutes. When you're done, repeat this four more times.

67

Try *Prompt #66* using a different genre. If you don't have a bunch of books in a different genre, visit your local library and snag a stack from the romance or mystery genre. Literary fiction also works well, and this exercise is a lot of fun if you use the last line of a poem.

68

Your character wakes up to find that he/she is the last person on earth. What happens next?

69

Your character is a novice monk who has been sent to a village far from the abbey. Rumors about the village have circulated for years, talk of witches and sorcery. Describe what your character sees while approaching the town. Describe an encounter with a farmer on the edge of the village.

70

Your character visits the National Gallery of Art and gets separated from the group. He/she has wandered into a room with only one large painting on the wall, and no other visitors. Your character is drawn toward the painting. Then, the man in the painting moves.

71

Your character lives in a suburban complex built for upper-middle-class families, far from the rabble. Rather than hire unwashed undesirables, your character's family purchases a housekeeping robot to clean and cook. Write about a morning for your character as the house gets ready for work and school.

72

Write prompt 71 from the robot's perspective.

73

Five years ago, an army of aliens invaded Earth, destroying most of the major cities and enslaving hundreds of millions of humans. Your character lives in the middle of Nebraska, and has escaped the notice of the aliens—so far. One morning, your character is in the field tending to the family crops when he/she finds an alien scouting ship, which has landed in the middle of the field. The cockpit is empty, but the corn behind your character is rustling.

74

A young girl goes to the circus with her family. She is soon separated from the group, and finds herself in a small tent by herself. As she begins to look around, she sees that there are a number of cages, each with a creature more unusual than the last.

75

Creating Cool Creatures The crown-of-thorns starfish (or seastar), feeds on coral by climbing on top of it, pushing its stomach out of its body and onto the coral, and secreting digestive enzymes that help it absorb nutrients from the coral. The crown-of-thorns is one of the largest starfish in the world, and can grow to over a foot wide. They have long spines full of toxin. They have seen an increase in their population because some of their natural predators have been over-fished, and they are now wreaking havoc on large portions of the Great Barrier Reef.

Imagine a world where the crown-of-thorns starfish have decimated the Great Barrier Reef, and now have to travel on land in search of food. On land, they grow larger, as large as a man. Humans become their favorite prey. Write a scene in which a family of four is spending the day on the beach, and they are stalked by a crown-of-thorns starfish. How long can you sustain the suspense before the starfish claims its first victim? Does anyone survive?

76

Lamarckism is the scientific theory that an organism will pass on characteristics gained during its lifetime to its offspring. Although Lamarckism is often associated with Darwinism, it is considered by many to be a less than solid scientific theory.

Imagine a world where people can modify their appearance or bodies and pass that on to their offspring. Write about a couple who go through a series of body modifications in the hopes of passing these changes on to their offspring.

77

Your character books a 'flight' with a time travel tourism company, and then something goes horribly wrong. He finds himself 20 years in the past without his tour guide, and without a way to get home. Who does he meet? How does he explain his situation? How will he get back home? Write in first-person POV.

78

Now write prompt #77 from the perspective of a person who has met the time-traveling tourist. Do they see the tourist 'arrive'? How do they react to what he has to say? Write in first-person POV.

79

Now write prompt #77 from the perspective of the scientist who eventually invents time travel tourism. The character from prompt #77 has found the scientist, who has no idea he will eventually invent a method of time travel. How do they react to what he has to say? Does this visit affect the scientist's understanding of their work up until now? Write in first-person POV.

80

Famous 16th Century astronomer Tycho Brahe lost part of his nose in a duel over the legitimacy of a mathematic formula. Neither he nor his opponent could prove their case, so they dueled to decide the matter.

Write about a duel (your choice of weapon) between two men/women of science who have decided to settle an intellectual matter with physical violence. Focus on fleshing out the two characters. There might be other people observing, but concentrate your energy on the duelists. What kind of man/woman would settle a matter of science in such a non-scientific way? Describe the duel itself, and then the outcome. Is the matter simply settled between them personally, or does the duel itself change some law of the Universe?

81

A **zoophyte** is an animal that looks like a plant (such as a sea anemone), but for many renaissance and medieval herbalists and doctors, the word was used to describe a plant that bore animals as its fruit. Perhaps the most famous example of this is the Vegetable Lamb of Tartary, a plant that was reputed to grow a fully-formed lamb, made of flesh and blood and attached to it by an umbilical cord. Some people believed that it would die with the plant or if removed from it, while others believed that it could be 'harvested' alive.

First, brainstorm a quick list of six plants and six animals. Take no more than a minute to finish both. Then roll a pair of dice to match one item from each list. Write about your newly created zoophyte for five minutes. Where does it grow? What kind of nutrition does it require? What does it look like, and what kind of noises does it make? Now do this three more times.

82

Choose one of your new zoophytes from #81. Your character comes across this zoophyte, which he/she has never been before. Describe the discovery.

83

Choose a zoophyte from #81. Your character is on the hunt for this zoophyte. What properties does it have that make it valuable to a hunter? What happens?

84

Choose a zoophyte from #81. Your character grows/raises this type of zoophyte in a greenhouse. One night, he/she hears someone breaking into the greenhouse...

85

The Myth of Orpheus and Eurydice: Eurydice is bitten by a snake on her wedding day and dies. Her husband, Orpheus, goes into the underworld and begs Hades to let Eurydice go. Hades agrees, on one condition: Orpheus must lead her out and not look back. Unfortunately, the closer he gets to the surface, the less certain he is that she is still behind him. Just before they are free, he looks back and she disappears forever. (*cont. next page*)

Let's put a twist on this myth. What if Orpheus (or your character) has to bring someone to Hades (or another underworld figure of your choice) as a trade for his wife? Write about their descent into the underworld. Is the traded person aware of the exchange, or has he/she been tricked?

Inspiration note for this prompt: Orpheus was famous for playing beautiful music, and in fact his music was part of the reason why the gods of the underworld allowed him to try and retrieve his wife.

86

A lot of fantasy and science fiction involves a journey. Your character is far from home, and daydreams about being back there. Who has he/she left behind? What does home look/smell/sound like? Will he/she ever be able to go back?

87

Your character sits down in front of his/her loom one morning with a new batch of wool, just purchased from the market. The old crone who sold your character the wool asked a premium price, and swore that it had magical properties. As your character weaves, the rhythm of the shuttle moving back and forth lulls him/her into a trance. What happens next?

88

"The sky was blue, but the breeze brought with it the stench of corpses and the ever-louder grinding of machines."

89

You character is a sellsword who finds two orphans in the burnt out shell of a village. A week before, an army had come through, burned the village and put all the villagers to the sword.

Right away, your character can tell that these children are strange. They both have pitch black hair, pale skin and ice blue eyes.

90

"She kept digging. It seemed like she'd always been digging. But she could tell she was close: the talisman around her neck was glowing brighter with every fistful of dirt."

91

Your character is a thief and a pickpocket. He has just returned to his den (a room in a boarding house, a cave in the woods, your choice) with his haul for the day. He sifts through his newly acquired treasure, and finds a mysterious black bag that he doesn't remember stealing.

92

For nearly two decades, humans have been embroiled in an inter-galactic war with an alien race. Your character is a crewman/crewwoman on a spaceship, and the ship has just been spotted by an enemy armada. Your character's ship is so outnumbered, there is only one choice: run! Ahead is an asteroid field, and the alien fleet is closing in on three sides.

93

Write #92 from the perspective of the captain.

94

Write #92 from the perspective of the alien captain

95

Scientists at the University of South Carolina have developed a form of cotton which is highly conductive. They believe they will soon be able to develop clothing that can generate energy for devices like phones and tablets, and even store energy like a battery.

Your character is a mercenary with a war conglomerate, and imbedded deep in a hostile country. Your character's weapons are powered by batteries built into his/her clothing, which are kinetically charged through movement. The battery is running low, and the enemy is closing in.

96

Your character is a scientist in a deep-sea exploration and research facility. He/she works in the main building, which is connected by pipelines, cables and tracks to outposts where scientists and miners conduct studies, and collect precious metals and minerals.

A stock train has not returned from a supply run to one of the furthest outposts. Write about your character's attempt to find out what happened.

97

"She turned the page, and was stunned to see the writing begin to glow."

98

Your character is a henchman for an evil queen. Tonight, she plans to sacrifice a child during a ritual that will give her immortality. One problem: Your character has just lost the baby. What happens next?

99

A lichgate (sometimes licht-gate) is a gate to a churchyard with a roof and a bier where a corpse would be place to await an escort into the yard by a clergyman. A licht is an undead creature that often possesses supernatural powers.

Your character awakens under the lichgate in the dead of night. She does not recall how she got there, or why she's wearing a long, flowing white dress. She looks down to see that the white lilies in her hand are dead and dry.

100

Your character is on a boat in the middle of the ocean. Describe an encounter with a mermaid.

Now a merman.

Your character is a mermaid. Describe an encounter with a fishing boat.

~ 48 ~

101

"He blinked and drew a deep breath, and then plunged into the eerie red smoke."

Thank You!

Yes, you, writer. Thank you, for spending your hard-earned cash to purchase my book. I hope we got the juices flowing (insert lewdly winking emoticon here), and that you're now bursting with great stories.

As I said in the preface, I'm here to answer your questions, and I'm dying to read what you came up with. Please send an email my way (**LKeenerGrant@gmail.com**), or visit **https://editsbylauragrant.blogspot.com** to read more about writing, editing and what I had for breakfast.

I have several volumes planned, including more prompts for fantasy and sci-fi writers, prompts for supernatural and horror writers, and a book of visual prompts with Geoff Pratt, the cool dude who drew the cover art.

Speaking of cover art by cool dudes, visit Geoff's portfolio:

http://www.wix.com/geoffpratt/design#!drawings

Printed in Great Britain
by Amazon.co.uk, Ltd.,
Marston Gate.